The Teaching of

Reverence for Life

KARSH / OTTAWA

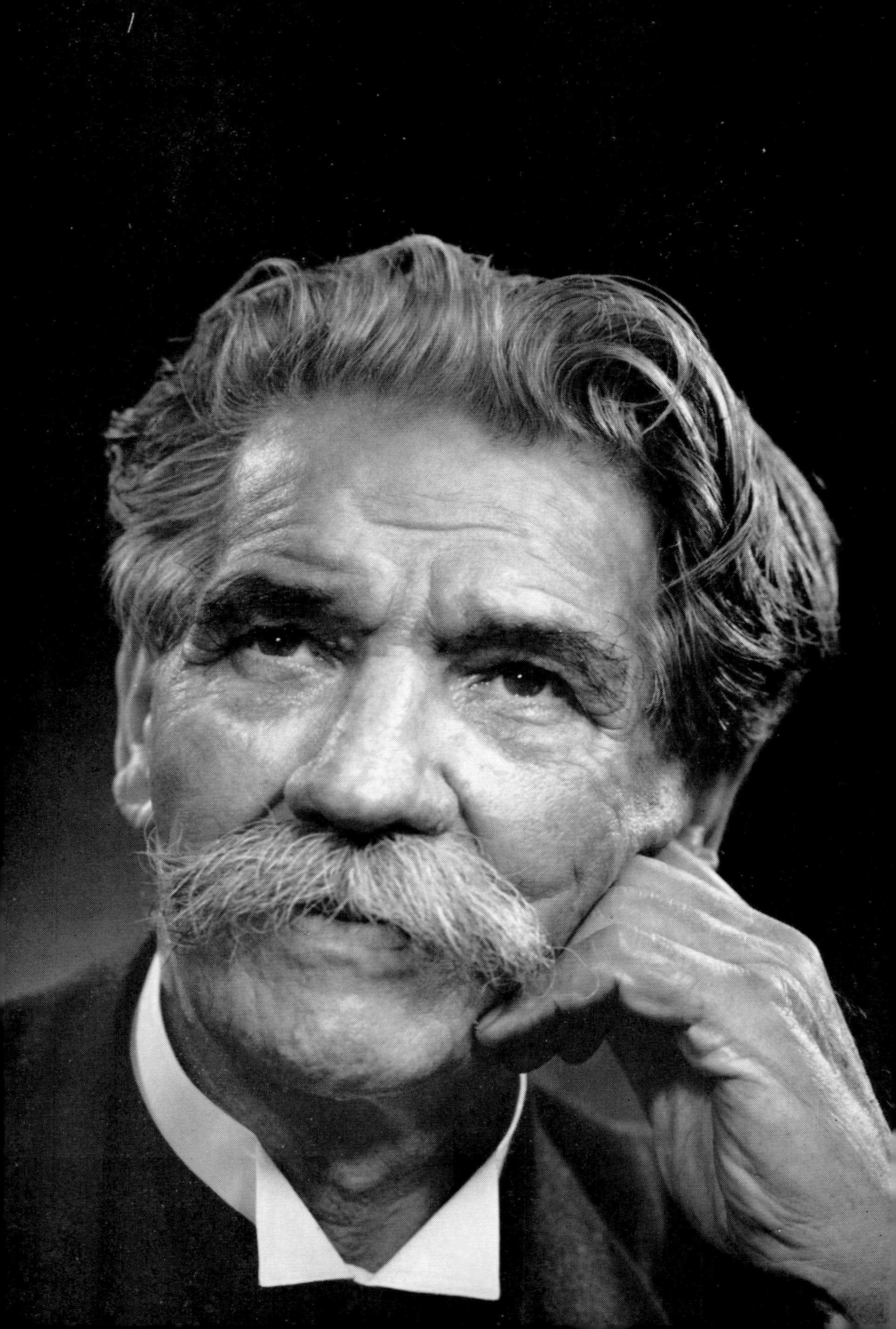

Albert Schweitzer
The Teaching of Reverence for Life

Translated from the German by Richard and Clara Winston

Holt, Rinehart and Winston

New York   Chicago   San Francisco

Contents

The Problem of Ethics

in the Advancement of

Human Consciousness   9

Ethical Culture   31

Man and Man   39

Man and Creature   47

Peace or Atomic War   53

An End to Atomic Weapons   59

The Problem of Ethics
in the Advancement of
Human Consciousness

WHAT do we mean when we speak of *ethics,* in a word borrowed from the Greek, and *morality,* in a word from the Latin? We mean right human conduct. The assumption is that we should be concerned not only with our own welfare but also with that of others, and with that of human society as a whole.

The first step in the evolution of ethics is an enlargement of the sense of solidarity with other human beings.

To the primitive, this solidarity has narrow limits. It is confined, first to his blood relations, and then to the members of his tribe, who represent to him the family enlarged. I speak from experience. I have such primitives in my hospital. If I ask an ambulatory patient to undertake some small service for a patient who must stay in bed, he will do it only if the bedridden patient belongs to his tribe. If that is not the case, he will answer me with wide-eyed innocence: "This man is not brother of me." Neither rewards nor threats will induce him to perform a service for such a stranger.

But as soon as man begins to reflect upon himself and his relationship to others, he becomes aware that men as such are his equals and his neighbors. In the course of gradual evolution he sees the circle of his responsibilities widening until he includes in it all human beings with whom he has any dealings.

Exponents of this more highly developed ethical view were: the Chinese thinker Lao-tse, born 604 B.C.; Kon-fu-tse (Confucius; 551-478 B.C.); Meng-tse (372-289 B.C.);

Chuang-tse (fourth century B.C.); and the Israelite prophets Amos, Hosea and Isaiah (seventh century B.C.). In the preaching of Jesus, as in that of Paul the Apostle, it is a fundamental tenet that man has a duty toward every other human being.

The idea of the brotherhood of all human beings is inherent in the metaphysics of the great religious systems of India, whether they be Brahmanism, Buddhism or Hinduism. Nevertheless it is no easy matter to apply this ethical conception. The great thinkers of India have not succeeded in eliminating the barriers between men created by the presence of different castes.

Zarathustra, who lived in Bactria (Eastern Persia) in the seventh century B.C., could not arrive at a conception of the brotherhood of all men because he felt compelled to make a distinction between those who believed in Ahura Mazda, the god of light, and those who did not believe. He demanded that the believers in Ahura Mazda regard these unbelievers as enemies, and treat them accordingly. In order to understand this attitude we should remind ourselves that the believers were the settled tribes of Bactria, who were beginning to live as peaceful tillers of the soil, while the nonbelievers remained nomadic marauders.

Plato, Aristotle and the other Greek philosophers of the classical age felt linked only to free Greeks who were above the cares of earning a livelihood. Those who did not belong to this aristocracy they considered an inferior breed in whom there was no need to take any further interest. It remained for the Stoics and Epicureans of the second era of Greek thought to affirm the equality of all men and to take an interest in man as such. The most noteworthy advocate of this new view was the Stoic Panaetius in the second century B.C. He was the prophet of humanism in the Greco-Roman world.

The idea of the brotherhood of all men played only a small part in antiquity. Philosophy, however, presented the case for humanitarianism as a concept recommended by reason, and this was of the utmost importance for the future.

Throughout history, the insight that we have a wider duty toward human beings as such has never attained the full dominance to which it is entitled. Down to our own times, it has been undermined by differences of race, religion and nationality, and we have not yet overcome the barriers of estrangement thus created between people.

It is interesting to see how the higher evolution of ethics is influenced by various philosophies of life. There are, after all, fundamental diversities in men's judgments of this world. Some world views take a positive attitude toward temporal values; they attribute importance to the things of this world and to existence in it. Other philosophies despise the world. They recommend indifference to everything that has to do with the temporal world. Affirmation of the world accords with our natural feelings. Such an attitude bids us feel at home in this world and be active in it. Negation of the world is unnatural; it orders us to live as strangers in the world, to which we nevertheless belong, and to abjure any action in the world as senseless.

By its very nature, ethics affirms the world. It calls for doing good actively and effectively. Hence we may say that affirmation of the world exerts a favorable influence upon the advancement of ethics, and that ethics has difficulty thriving in a climate of negation of the world. In the first case it can act according to its nature; in the second case it becomes artificial.

Negation of the world was taught by the thinkers of India, and by Christianity, in the ancient world and in the Middle Ages. Affirmation of the world was urged by the Chinese sages, the prophets of Israel, Zarathustra, and the European thinkers of the Renaissance and of modern times.

The Indian thinkers derive their negative attitude toward the world from their conviction that true Being is nonmaterial, immutable and eternal, whereas the nature of the material world is artificial, deceptive and transitory. To them the world, which we take as so real, is only an image, appearing in time and space, of nonmaterial Being. Man is caught in error if he accepts this illusion and the role he plays within it.

The only mode of conduct that complies with such a view is nonactivity. To a certain extent, nonactivity can be ethical. In being indifferent to the things of this world, man is free of the egoism that material interests arouse in him. What is more, nonactivity is connected with the idea of nonviolence. It preserves man from the danger of inflicting evil upon others by acts of violence.

The Indian philosophers of Brahmanism, of Samkhya and of Jainism praise nonviolence, which they call *ahimsa,* and regard it as the highest form of ethics. Buddha was also of this school of thought. But such a concept of ethics is faulty and incomplete. It permits man the egoistic attitude of being wholly concerned with his individual salvation, which he seeks to achieve by observing that nonactivity which accords with true knowledge. His compassion is not natural, for it derives from his metaphysical theories. Such compassion calls only for refraining from evil, not acting for good, which a natural feeling for what was right would inspire.

Only the kind of ethics that is linked with affirmation of the world can be natural and complete. When Indian thinkers become aware of the restricted nature of *ahimsa,* and feel impelled to seek a broader moral philosophy, they can do so only by making concessions to affirmation and the principle of activity. The Buddha, who rebelled against the callousness of Brahmanic doctrine and preached compassion, found it difficult to adhere to the principle of nonactivity. More than once he had to flout it, for he was unable to refrain from acts of loving-kindness and from recommending these to his disciples.

For centuries, a secret struggle has been waged in India between affirmation of the world and the principle of nonactivity. The issue is ethics. Hinduism, which is a religious movement directed against the excessive demands of Brahmanism, has given activity equal standing with nonactivity. The correlation of these two principles is set forth in the great didactic poem, the *Bhagavad-Gîtâ,* a part of the great Indian epic, *Mahâbhârata.*

The *Bhagavad-Gîtâ* accepts the world view of Brahmanism. It declares that the material world is only a seeming reality from which we should detach ourselves. That is, the world is no more than a stage play which God provides for Himself. The most natural conduct for man is to remain a spectator of that play.

But the *Bhagavad-Gîtâ* also seeks to allot man a place as an actor, in both senses, in this play. He is allowed to take part if he is properly aware of the play's true nature.

If he is cognizant that he is playing a part in the show that God has arranged for Himself, he is on the right path. For he is then active out of the same insight that prompts another to remain a pure onlooker. Both are knowers. But if he decides simply in favor of activity, if he considers the world real and wishes to accomplish something in it, he is entangled in error. Then his actions are folly. The thesis of the *Bhagavad-Gîtâ* can in no way satisfy the requirements of ethics. For the aim of ethics is improvement of the conditions of this world. The *Bhagavad-Gîtâ* does no more than provide a phan-

tom place for activistic ethics within the philosophy of
world-negation.

The Christianity of classical antiquity and of the Middle Ages professed renunciation of the world without insisting upon absolute nonactivity. This was tenable because Christian negation of the world differs from the negation advocated by Indian thinkers. It does not assume that the world we live in is an illusion. Rather, it sees this world as an imperfect one, which is destined to achieve perfection when the day of the Kingdom of God dawns. The Hebrew prophets first conceived the idea of the coming of a supernatural Kingdom of God. The same thought may also be found in the religion of Zarathustra.

Jesus, as well as John the Baptist, announced that the transformation of the material world into the Kingdom of God was near at hand. He called upon men to strive for the perfection that would be required of them for participation in the new existence in a new world. They were to renounce the things of this world in order to be free to dedicate themselves to the idea of the Good. The ethics of Jesus permits activity; it permits men to seek to accomplish all that they regard as good and requisite. Therein lies the difference between it and the doctrine of the Buddha, with which it shares the idea of compassion. The Buddha sets limits to compassionate activity. The ethics of Jesus, however, demands unlimited action in behalf of the Good.

The first Christians, including the Apostle Paul, expected that the Kingdom of God would come to replace the natural world within their very lifetime. Their hope was not fulfilled. In classical antiquity and well into the Middle Ages, Christians found themselves in the situation of having to live in the natural world without the sustaining hope of a speedy advent of the supernatural world.

Christianity was unable to decide fully in favor of affirmation of the world, although its active ethics was highly favorable to such a decision. No spirit of enthusiastic affirmation of the world arose, either in the early days of the Church or in the Middle Ages. Christians remained directed toward the hereafter.

Not until the Renaissance was there an awakening of a spirit of vigorous affirmation of the world. Since then, Christianity has been gradually entering into that spirit. Henceforth Christian ethics included not only the ideal of self-perfection formulated by Jesus, but also the other ideal of creating new and better material and spiritual conditions for man's existence in this world. Christian ethics now experienced a great revival because it had a goal for activity. The linking of Christianity and purposeful affirmation of the world produced the culture in which we live. To preserve and to perfect it is our task.

The Problem of Ethics

The ethical views of the Chinese sages and of Zarathustra were from the start inclined toward affirmation
of the world. They too contained within themselves the
requisite forces to shape an ethical philosophy of life.

At a certain state in its evolution, ethics strives to at-
tain greater depth. One sign of this is the urge to in-
vestigate the fundamental nature of the Good. Defin-
ing, listing and recommending various virtues and
duties no longer suffice; rather, ethical thought seeks to
determine what all these virtues have and are striving
for in common. In their search, the great Chinese sages
arrived at the conclusion that the common aim of all
ethical conduct is good will toward man. They extol
this as the fundamental virtue.

Even before Jesus, Hebrew ethics considered the
question of the highest commandment, which in itself
would comprehend keeping the whole of the Law.
Jesus, faithful to the tradition of the Jewish Scribes,
made Love the supreme commandment that includes all
others within itself.

Similarly, the thinkers of the schools of Stoics and
Epicureans, in the two first centuries of the Christian
era, pursued the path laid down by Panaetius, the
founder of the humanitarian ideal, and came to the
conclusion that love of man was the virtue of all virtues.
Among these were Seneca (c. 4 B.C. to A.D. 65), Epicte-
tus (50-138) and the Emperor Marcus Aurelius (121-
180). Their ethics basically corresponds to the views of

Chinese and Christian thinkers. Its striking feature is their conviction that thought, if it plunges deeply, arrives at the humanitarian ideal.

Since in the course of the first and second centuries after Christ Greco-Roman philosophy attained to the same ethical ideal as Christianity, the two streams of thought might have become aware of what they had in common. But this did not happen. They remained alien to one another. The circumstances which would have permitted mutual recognition did not exist. Greco-Roman philosophy, highly developed though it was, flourished only for a short time. It was the concern of a small upper class of the cultured. The common people ignored it.

Moreover, both movements were profoundly prejudiced toward one another. To the Greco-Roman thinker, Christianity, with its expectations of a supernatural world whose ruler was to be a Jew crucified in Jerusalem, seemed rank superstition. To the Christian thinker, the whole of Greco-Roman philosophy belonged to paganism; hence, if it was noticed at all, it was given short shrift.

Centuries later, however, the two nevertheless entered into relation with one another. When in the sixteenth and seventeenth centuries Christianity began to familiarize itself with the spirit of world-affirmation the Renaissance had bequeathed to European thought, it also discovered the profound ethical views developed by Late Stoicism and Epicureanism in the first two centuries A.D. Christian thinkers found to their surprise that those philosophers had also subscribed to Jesus' commandment of Love, which they had represented as a truth commended by reason. Here was telling proof that the fundamental ideas of ethics are truths both revealed by religion and confirmed by philosophy.

Among the most eminent of the thinkers who consciously aligned themselves both with Christianity and Late Stoicism were Erasmus of Rotterdam (1465-1536) and Hugo Grotius (1583-1645). These men undertook to devise principles of ethical justice which could be observed by all nations in peace and in war.

Both Christian and philosophical ethics were seized by an ardor for action. With common accord they took stock of the world. They cried out against the glaring injustices they saw around them, against cruelty and baneful superstition. In the eighteenth century, torture was abolished, the horrors of the witch trials came to an end. Inhuman laws were replaced by milder ones. A program of reform unique in the history of humanity was undertaken, and in the elation of the discovery that the commandment of Love is also supported by reason, the program was carried out.

To demonstrate the reasonableness of love of neighbor, Jeremy Bentham (1748-1832) and others resorted to the argument of its utility. As they present it, love of neighbor is only an extension of egotism, properly understood. The welfare of the individual and of society can be secured only by a degree of altruism. Men should be prepared for such altruism in their intercourse with their fellows.

This is a somewhat superficial view of the nature of ethical conduct. It is rejected by, among others, Immanuel Kant (1724-1804) and the Scottish philosopher David Hume (1711-1776). Kant, who wishes to see the dignity of ethics unimpaired, will not allow the question of utility even to enter the picture. According to his doctrine of the categorical imperative, ethics can make absolute demands. Our conscience, he declares, discriminates between good and evil. This alone should guide our actions. The moral law immanent in us assures us beyond doubt that we do not merely share the world of time and space around us, but that we are also citizens of a spiritual world.

Hume, for his part, rejects utilitarian ethics on the grounds of human experience. He analyzes the basis of ethics and comes to the conclusion that ethical conduct is principally a matter of sympathy, of fellow-feeling. Nature, he argues, has endowed us with this ability to share experientially in the lot of others. We experience the joys, the sorrows and the sufferings of others as if they were our own. We are, in Hume's image, strings that vibrate in sympathy with others. Natural good will prompts us to help our neighbors and to wish to contribute to their welfare as well as to that of society.

Since Hume, philosophy—if we except Friedrich Nietzsche (1844-1900)—takes it for granted that ethics is primarily a matter of fellow-feeling and of helpful action flowing out of that natural sympathy.

But natural ethics, profound though it is, soon falls into a quandary. How is it to determine and delimit its responsibilities, so that natural concern for our own well-being will be properly related to concern for the well-being of others?

Hume does not explore this problem. Neither do any of his contemporaries, and later philosophers seemed also to avoid the question. Perhaps an intimation of the difficulties facing them has made them cautious.

The fact is that the questions that arise out of such elementary ethics are truly imposing and cannot be readily dealt with. It is impossible to frame a natural system of ethics in clearly formulated commandments and prohibitions. It is entirely subjective. The individual must decide for himself how far he will go in self-sacrificing altruism. He is not exempted from acts of self-sacrifice that he may regard as excessive, even if such acts should bring him dire disadvantages. His conscience is never allowed to rest. Operating under such a natural mode of ethics, a clean conscience becomes a will-o'-the-wisp.

In many life-situations, the ethics of altruism, calls for stringent decisions from those who wish to follow it. Men in charge of business enterprises can seldom plume themselves on having compassionately given a job to the person who needed it most, rather than to the person best qualified. But woe to the man who concludes on the basis of such examples that compassion need not play a part in his decisions!

As we reflect upon the problem of altruism, we find ourselves enlarging the circle of our ethical activity. We begin to perceive that ethics deals not only with people, but also with creatures. Even as we, they have the desire for well-being, the endurance of suffering, and the horror of annihilation. Those who have retained an unblunted moral sensibility find it natural to share concern with the fate of all living creatures. The thoughtful cannot help recognizing that kindly conduct toward nonhuman life is a natural requirement of ethics. That men hesitate to practice this law has its reasons. In fact, concern with the lot of all living creatures with which we have dealings plunges us into more variegated and more confusing conflicts than concern restricted to human beings. The novel and tragic element is that in this field we are continually facing the decision between killing or letting live. The farmer cannot raise all the animals that are born in his herd. He will keep only as many as he can feed and raise with assurance of profit. Moreover, in many cases we are compelled to sacrifice some living creatures in order to save others threatened by it.

Whoever picks up a bird fallen from the nest finds himself having to kill small living creatures in order to feed his ward. Such action is totally arbitrary. By what right does he sacrifice a multitude of lives for the sake of a single one? Man behaves with the same arbitrariness when he destroys certain animal pests in order to protect other animals he favors.

Each of us must therefore decide whether to condemn living creatures to suffering or death out of inescapable necessity, and thus to incur guilt. Some atonement for that guilt can be found by the man who pledges himself to neglect no opportunity to succor creatures in distress. How much farther along would we be if men showed some concern for other forms of life and renounced all the evils they inflict upon so many living creatures from sheer thoughtlessness. We must in our time make it our special task to struggle against the antihuman traditions and inhuman emotions that are still too much in our midst.

As examples of such inhuman habits which our civilization and our feelings should no longer countenance, we may mention bullfights and hunting with beaters.

An ethics that does not also consider our relation to the world of creatures is incomplete. The struggle against inhumanity must be waged wholly and continually. We must reach the stage at which killing for sport will be felt as a disgrace to our civilization.

There is another great difference between the ethical situation of the present and that of the past. The moral philosopher of today must admit that he can no longer expect to found his ethics upon a world view inherently in keeping with it. In the past, men could believe that ethical behavior accorded with what they knew to be the true nature of the universal will to life, as this was revealed in the created world. Not only the higher religions, but also the rationalistic philosophy of the seventeenth and eighteenth centuries hold this view.

The fact is, however, that their optimistic interpretation of the world was really the fruit, rather than the germ, of their ethics. Those moral philosophers had committed the highly human error of describing the universal will to life in terms of feeling and judging.

In the course of the nineteenth and twentieth centuries, thinking men concerned solely with seeking truth were forced to admit that ethics has nothing to gain from a true understanding of the universe. The advancement of knowledge takes the form of an ever more precise understanding of the laws of phenomena. Science benefits us in that it enables us to put the energies available in the universe to use. But we are more and more led to abandon hope of being able to understand the meaning of phenomena.

Can altruism be justified within the terms of a world view? Ethical thinkers have constantly endeavored to do this. They have never succeeded. When they thought they had done so, they had in fact been constructing only the requisite naïvely optimistic world view that would accord with their ethical principles. However, a philosophy that proceeds from truth has to confess that no spirit of loving-kindness is at work in the phenome-

nal world. The universe provides us with the dreary
spectacle of manifestations of the will to live continually
opposed to each other. One life preserves itself by fight-
ing and destroying other lives. The world is horror in
splendor, meaninglessness in meaning, sorrow in joy.

Ethics is not in tune with this phenomenal world, but
in rebellion against it. It is the manifestation of a spirit
that desires to be different from the spirit that mani-
fests itself in the universe.

If we attempt to comprehend the phenomenal world
as it is and deduce principles of conduct from it, we are
doomed to skepticism and pessimism. On the contrary,
ethics is an act of spiritual independence on our part.

Early ethical thought had to create a world view in
keeping with its values. It postulated a spirit that dom-
inated the phenomenal world, and that, imperfect
though it was, strove to achieve perfection. Our ethical
strivings in the present world had meaning in view of
that hoped-for goal.

But once ethical thought has come to see that concern
for other wills to live is mandatory for us as human beings; that intellectually advanced men feel that concern
and cannot escape it—once ethical thought reaches that
insight, it has become completely autonomous. Henceforth, the fact that we possess only an imperfect and
quite unsatisfactory understanding of the universe no
longer seems so troubling. We possess understanding of
the conduct our natures require. Faithful to that understanding, we proceed on our way.

The elemental fact, present in our consciousness every moment of our existences, is: I am life that wills to live, in the midst of life that wills to live. The mysterious fact of my will to live is that I feel a mandate to behave with sympathetic concern toward all the wills to live which exist side by side with my own. The essence of Goodness is: Preserve life, promote life, help life to achieve its highest destiny. The essence of Evil is: Destroy life, harm life, hamper the development of life.

The fundamental principle of ethics, then, is reverence for life. All the goodness one displays toward a living organism is, at bottom, helping it to preserve and further its existence.

In the main, reverence for life dictates the same sort of behavior as the ethical principle of love. But reverence for life contains within itself the rationale of the commandment to love, and it calls for compassion for all creature life.

It should also be observed that the ethics of love governs only our conduct toward others, not toward ourselves. Truthfulness, which is a fundamental element of the ethical personality, cannot be deduced from it. But the reverence we should manifest toward our own existence commands us to remain always true to ourselves, to reject all the distortions of our true selves that we might be tempted to practice in one situation or another, and never to slacken in the struggle to remain wholly truthful.

The Problem of Ethics

Only the ethics of reverence for life is complete. It is so in every respect. The ethics that deals only with the conduct of man toward his fellow men can be exceedingly profound and vital. But it remains incomplete. Thus it was inevitable that man's intellect should ultimately have reached the point of being offended by the heartless treatment of other living creatures, which had hitherto been considered acceptable, and should have demanded that ethics include them within its merciful purview. Ethical thought was slow and hesitant about taking this demand seriously. Only in recent times has visible progress been made along these lines, and only recently has the world begun to pay some regard to the undertaking.

But already the world is beginning to recognize that the ethics of reverence for life, which requires kindness toward all living organisms, accords with the natural feelings of thinking men.

By ethical conduct toward all creatures, we enter into a spiritual relationship with the universe.

In the universe, the will to live is in conflict with itself. In us, it seeks to be at peace with itself.

In the universe, the will to live is a fact; in us, it is a revelation.

The mind commands us to be different from the universe. By reverence for life we become, in profound, elemental and vital fashion, devout.

Ethical Culture

WE WHO ARE heirs of a complex civilization are charged with one major historical task: to aid the world in achieving true culture. It is up to us to make the light of truly humanitarian culture shine throughout the world.

Once there are many rather than few to bring humanitarianism to bear upon reality in thought and action, humanitarianism will cease to be regarded as a sentimental notion and will become what it ought to be: a yeast in the convictions of individuals and of society. Reverence for life, arising when intelligence operates upon the will to live, contains within itself affirmation of the universe and of life. Intricately intertwined with such affirmation, it contains the principles of ethics. Reverence for life is, inevitably, forever concerned with the idea of ethical culture.

The principle of reverence for life rejects relativism. It recognizes as good only the preserving and benefiting of life: any injury to, and destruction of, life, unless it is imposed upon us by fate, is regarded as evil. It does not have a large stock of compromises between ethics and necessity, on which it is always ready to draw. In every case we must decide ourselves to what extent we may remain ethical and to what extent we will have to bow to the necessity of harming and destroying life, and thereby incurring the guilt of such actions. The more we act in accordance with the principle of reverence for life, the more we are gripped by the desire to preserve and benefit life.

The principle of reverence for life includes an elemental sense of responsibility to which we must submit with all our being. There are forces active within that principle which cause us to refine our individual, social and political attitudes.

Reverence for life means being seized by the unfathomable, forward-moving will which is inherent in all Being. It raises us above perception of the world of objects and makes us into the tree that is safe from drought because it is planted by the water.

The man who subscribes to this ethic is soon made to feel, by its demands upon him, the fire glowing within the abstract phrase, "reverence for life." Its edict is the rule of universal love. This is the ethics of Jesus reinforced by reason.

Through it man gives value to his existence, no matter what its circumstances or what paths he must tread.

Born out of inner necessity, this ethics scarcely depends upon cerebral effort. It can do without an infallible philosophical system. It transcends the question of what becomes of the ethical man's endeavors to preserve, promote and intensify life within the total movement of the universe. Even if this effort of preserving and perfecting life is almost infinitesimal when matched against the destructive forces nature may unleash at any moment, the ethical spirit is not deflected from its course. It seeks a field of action and in so doing it is free to ignore the matter of success or failure. The very fact that man espouses such an ethic, that he is filled with reverence and concern for life, is in itself fraught with significance for the universe.

In all respects, the universe remains mysterious to man. But even if we must despair of comprehending the phenomenal world, we need not confront the problem of life in utter perplexity. Reverence for life sets up a relationship between our minds and the universe that is independent of intellectual understanding. Reverence for life leads us by inner necessity through the dark vale of resignation up to the bright highlands of ethical affirmation of life and the universe.

Three kinds of progress are significant for culture: progress in knowledge and technology; progress in the socialization of man; progress in spirituality. The last is the most important.

As soon as man does not take his existence for granted, but beholds it as something unfathomably mysterious, thought begins. This phenomenon has been repeated time and time again in the history of the human race. Ethical affirmation of life is the intellectual act by which man ceases simply to live at random and begins to concern himself reverently with his own life, so that he may realize its true value.

Thought has a dual task to accomplish: to lead us out of a naïve and into a profounder affirmation of life and the universe; and to help us progress from ethical impulses to a rational system of ethics.

In embracing ethical culture, the individual is also giving the best of his mind and will to the service of his country and of humanity.

Energy is a noiseless force. It is there, and it operates. True ethics begins where the use of words ceases.

We must think things out afresh and arrive at a philosophy of life that contains the ideals of true culture. If only we began again to reflect upon ethics and our spiritual relationship to the world, we would be on the road that leads from barbarism to culture.

For centuries, seafarers kept their course as best they could by the stars. But eventually they rose above the imperfections of this method by discovering that the magnetic needle pointed north in response to a constantly operative force. Thereafter they found their way safely in darkest night upon the remotest seas.

The progress we must seek in a perfected ethics is of that kind. As long as our ethics is a matter of duties and virtues, we are finding our direction by the stars; however brilliantly they gleam, they are nevertheless only uncertain guides that, moreover, are easily concealed by a rising fog. On a stormy night they are no help. Our present situation is just that. But if we develop an ethics based on a conscious and rational idea of reverence for life, we have found a more trustworthy guide which will serve all humanity. We will then be well on our way to true ethical progress.

When in the spring the withered gray of the fields gives way to a carpet of green, this is because millions of shoots are springing up anew from the roots. Our age must achieve spiritual renewal. It can do so only in one way: the masses of the people must reflect upon the nature of true goodness. Out of such reflection, new principles and ideas will inevitably arise. As the trees bear the same fruit anew year after year, so from generation to generation all worthwhile ideas must be born anew in the thinking of mankind.

A new renaissance must come, perhaps a greater one than brought us forth from the Middle Ages: the great renaissance in which mankind discovers that ethical action is the supreme truth and the supreme utilitarianism. By it mankind will be liberated from the poverty-stricken pragmatism in which it has been limping along.

All I desire is to be one who prepares the way for this renaissance. I am bold enough to believe in a new mankind because I am convinced that the principles of humanitarianism, hitherto regarded only as noble sentiments, are founded upon a generally communicable philosophy of life, the fruit of simple, straightforward thinking. Consequently humanitarianism commands a persuasiveness it did not have in the past; it is now capable of dealing energetically with reality and winning respect in the world as it is.

Man and Man

No HUMAN being is ever totally and permanently a stranger to another human being. Man belongs to man. Man is entitled to man. Large and small circumstances break in to dispel the estrangement we impose upon ourselves in daily living, and to bring us close to one another, man to man. We obey a law of proper reserve; but that law is bound to give way at times to the rule of cordiality.

There is much coldness among men because we do not dare to be as cordial as we really are.

Just as the wave cannot exist for itself, but must always participate in the swell of the ocean, so we can never experience our lives by ourselves, but must always share the experiencing of life that takes place all around us.

The ethics of reverence for life requires that all of us somehow and in something shall act as men toward other men. Those who in their occupations have nothing to give as men to other men, and who possess nothing else they can give away, must sacrifice some of their time and leisure, no matter how sparse it may be. Choose an avocation, the ethics of reverence for life commands—an inconspicuous, perhaps a secret avocation. Open your eyes and seek another human being in need of a little time, a little friendliness, a little company, a little work. It may be a lonely, an embittered, a sick or an awkward person for whom you can do something, to whom you can mean something. Perhaps it will be an old person or a child. Or else a good cause needs volunteer workers, people who can give up a free evening or run errands. Who can list all the uses to which that precious working capital called man can be put? Do not lose heart, even if you must wait a bit before finding the right thing, even if you must make several attempts.

Be prepared for disappointments also! But do not abandon your quest for the avocation, for that sideline in which you can act as a man for other men. There is one waiting for you, if only you really want it. . . .

This is the message of true ethics to those who have only a little time and a little humanity to give. Fortunate are those who listen. Their own humanity will be enriched, whereas in moral isolation from their fellow men, their store of humanity would dwindle.

Each of us, no matter what our position and occupation, must try to act in such a way as to further true humanity.

Those who have the opportunity to serve others freely and personally should see this good fortune as grounds for humility. The practice of humility will strengthen their will to be of service.

No one has the right to take for granted his own advantages over others in health, in talents, in ability, in success, in a happy childhood or congenial home conditions. One must pay a price for all these boons. What one owes in return is a special responsibility for other lives.

All through the world, there is a special league of those who have known anxiety and physical suffering. A mysterious bond connects those marked by pain. They know the terrible things man can undergo; they know the longing to be free of pain. Those who have been liberated from pain must not think they are now completely free again and can calmly return to life as it was before. With their experience of pain and anxiety, they must help alleviate the pain and anxiety of others, insofar as that lies within human powers. They must bring release to others as they received release.

He who has experienced good in his life must feel the obligation to dedicate some of his own life in order to alleviate suffering.

Technical progress, extension of knowledge, do indeed represent progress, but not in fundamentals. The essential thing is that we become more finely and deeply human.

Doing and suffering, we have the chance to prove our mettle as people who have painfully fought our way to the peace that can never be attained by reason alone.

We are headed right when we trust subjective thinking and look to it to yield the insights and truths we need for living.

Just as white light consists of colored rays, so reverence for life contains all the components of ethics: love, kindliness, sympathy, empathy, peacefulness, power to forgive.

We must all bid ourselves to be natural and to express our unexpressed gratitude. That will mean more sunlight in the world, and more strength for the good. Let us be careful not to incorporate bitter phrases about the world's ingratitude into our philosophy of life. There is much water flowing underground which does not well up from springs. We can take comfort from that. But we ourselves should try to be water that finds its way to a spring, where people can gratefully quench their thirst.

Thoughtlessness is to blame for the paucity of gratitude in our lives. Resist this thoughtlessness. Tell yourself to feel and express gratitude in a natural way. It will make you happy, and you will make others happy.

The man who has the courage to examine and to judge himself makes progress in kindness.

It is a hard fight for all of us to become truly peaceable.

Right thinking leaves room for the heart to add its word.

Constant kindness can accomplish much. As the sun makes ice melt, kindness causes misunderstandings, mistrust and hostility to evaporate.

The kindness a man pours out into the world affects the hearts and the minds of men.

Where there is energy, it will have effects. No ray of sunlight is lost; but the green growth that sunlight awakens needs time to sprout, and the sower is not always destined to witness the harvest. All worthwhile accomplishment is acting on faith.

The one thing that truly matters is that we struggle for light to be within us. Each feels the others' struggle, and when a man has light within him it shines out upon others.

The great secret is to go through life as an unspoiled human being. This can be done by one who does not cavil at men and facts, but who in all experiences is thrown back upon himself and looks within himself for the explanation of whatever happens to him.

None of us knows what he accomplishes and what he gives to humanity. That is hidden from us, and should remain so. Sometimes we are allowed to see just a little of it, so we will not be discouraged. The effects of energy are mysterious in all realms.

The epithet "mature," when applied to people, has always struck me as somewhat uncomplimentary. It carries overtones of spiritual impoverishment, stunting, blunting of sensibilities. What we usually call maturity in a person is a form of resigned reasonableness. A man acquires it by modeling himself on others and bit by bit abandoning the ideas and convictions that were precious to him in his youth. He once believed in the victory of truth; now he no longer does. He believed in humanity; that is over. He believed in the Good; that is over. He eagerly sought justice; that is over. He trusted in the power of kindness and peaceableness; that is over. He could become enthusiastic; that is over. In order to steer more safely through the perils and storms of life, he has lightened his boat. He has thrown overboard goods that he considered dispensable. But the ballast he dumped was actually his food and drink. Now he skims more lightly over the waves, but he is hungry and parched.

Adults are only too partial to the sorry task of warning youth that some day they will view most of the things that now inspire their hearts and minds as mere illusions. But those who have a deeper experience of life take another tone. They exhort youth to try to preserve throughout their lives the ideas that inspire them. In youthful idealism man perceives the truth. In youthful idealism he possesses riches that should not be bartered for anything on earth.

Those who vow to do good should not expect people to clear the stones from their path on this account. They must expect the contrary: that others will roll great boulders down upon them. Such obstacles can be overcome only by the kind of strength gained in the very struggle. Those who merely resent obstacles will waste whatever force they have.

Man and Creature

THE ethics of reverence for life makes no distinction between higher and lower, more precious and less precious lives. It has good reasons for this omission. For what are we doing, when we establish hard and fast gradations in value between living organisms, but judging them in relation to ourselves, by whether they seem to stand closer to us or farther from us. This is a wholly subjective standard. How can we know what importance other living organisms have in themselves and in terms of the universe?

In making such distinctions, we are apt to decide that there are forms of life which are worthless and may be stamped out without its mattering at all. This category may include anything from insects to primitive peoples, depending on circumstances.

To the truly ethical man, all life is sacred, including forms of life that from the human point of view may seem to be lower than ours. He makes distinctions only from case to case, and under pressure of necessity, when he is forced to decide which life he will sacrifice in order to preserve other lives. In thus deciding from case to case, he is aware that he is proceeding subjectively and arbitrarily, and that he is accountable for the lives thus sacrificed.

The man who is guided by the ethics of reverence for life stamps out life only from inescapable necessity, never from thoughtlessness. He seizes every occasion to feel the happiness of helping living things and shielding them from suffering and annihilation.

Whenever we harm any form of life, we must be clear about whether it was really necessary to do so. We must not go beyond the truly unavoidable harm, not even in seemingly insignificant matters. The farmer who mows down a thousand flowers in his meadow, in order to feed his cows, should be on guard, as he turns homeward, not to decapitate some flower by the roadside, just by way of thoughtlessly passing the time. For then he sins against life without being under the compulsion of necessity.

Those who carry out scientific experiments with animals, in order to apply the knowledge gained to the alleviation of human ills, should never reassure themselves with the generality that their cruel acts serve a useful purpose. In each individual case they must ask themselves whether there is a real necessity for imposing such a sacrifice upon a living creature. They must try to reduce the suffering insofar as they are able. It is inexcusable for a scientific institution to omit anesthesia in order to save time and trouble. It is horrible to subject animals to torment merely in order to demonstrate to students phenomena that are already familiar.

The very fact that animals, by the pain they endure in experiments, contribute so much to suffering humanity, should forge a new and unique kind of solidarity between them and us. For that reason alone it is incumbent upon each and every one of us to do all possible good to nonhuman life.

When we help an insect out of a difficulty, we are only trying to compensate for man's ever-renewed sins against other creatures. Wherever animals are impressed into the service of man, every one of us should be mindful of the toll we are exacting. We cannot stand idly by and see an animal subjected to unnecessary harshness or deliberate mistreatment. We cannot say it is not our business to interfere. On the contrary, it is our duty to intervene in the animal's behalf.

No one may close his eyes and pretend that the suffering that he does not see has not occurred. We must not take the burden of our responsibility lightly. When abuse of animals is widespread, when the bellowing of thirsty animals in cattle cars is heard and ignored, when cruelty still prevails in many slaughterhouses, when animals are clumsily and painfully butchered in our kitchens, when brutish people inflict unimaginable torments upon animals and when some animals are exposed to the cruel games of children, all of us share in the guilt.

As the housewife who has scrubbed the floor sees to it that the door is shut, so that the dog does not come in and undo all her work with his muddy paws, so religious and philosophical thinkers have gone to some pains to see that no animals enter and upset their systems of ethics.

It would seem as if Descartes, with his theory that

animals have no souls and are mere machines which only seem to feel pain, had bewitched all of modern philosophy. Philosophy has totally evaded the problem of man's conduct toward other organisms. We might say that philosophy has played a piano of which a whole series of keys were considered untouchable.

To the universal ethics of reverence for life, pity for animals, so often smilingly dismissed as sentimentality, becomes a mandate no thinking person can escape.

The time will come when public opinion will no longer tolerate amusements based on the mistreatment and killing of animals. The time will come, but when? When will we reach the point that hunting, the pleasure in killing animals for sport, will be regarded as a mental aberration? When will all the killing that necessity imposes upon us be undertaken with sorrow?

Peace or Atomic War

SINCE it is obvious that war in our time would be an unmitigated catastrophe, everything must be done to prevent it. In the last two wars we have been guilty of unspeakable inhumanity, and in the future war we would go on in the same vein. These horrors in which we have shared should have awakened us to the necessity of building an age in which there will be no more wars.

There are still many people in the world who do not understand that the atomic weapons we have at our disposal are so terrible that we cannot even consider waging a war with them. Such people live from day to day without giving thought to the danger to peace.

Even today there are still glorifiers of war. They still think of war in glamorous and idealized terms, as somehow hallowed by enthusiasm or self-defense. They leave out of consideration the toll war takes of millions of human lives. They ought to walk over a war cemetery with its thousands and thousands of crosses, and mull over the question of why the men buried together there had to suffer and die. A new kind of patriotism must arise; the new patriot must be able to feel more humanly and see farther than patriots of the past.

The point upon which our minds must fix from now on, for all the future, must be this: that questions dividing nations can no longer be adjudicated by warfare, but must be solved be peaceful negotiation. War has become something out of the question. Before this era, when weapons still had limited effects, it was possible to ridicule pacifism as utopianism. But in the present age of weapons that can annihilate millions of people in a single assault, and simultaneously poison the atmosphere with deadly radiation, peace has become an urgent necessity.

We should bless those men among us who are the spokesmen for peace, who are truly concerned with the coming of peace. People must be taught to honor the ideal of humanitarianism. That above all is essential. That is spiritual politics, which must be pursued side by side with all political planning and acting. Such politics will create spiritual links among the nations.

At the moment we have the choice between two dangerous courses. The one consists in continuing the senseless armaments race in atomic weapons, with the concomitant peril of an inevitable and imminent atomic war. The other consists in renouncing atomic weapons, in the faith that the peoples of East and West will learn to live in peace with one another. The first course holds out no chance for a salutary future. The second does. We must choose the second course.

The theory that peace can be maintained by the mutual deterrence of constantly increasing atomic armaments can no longer be entertained nowadays, when the danger of war is so grave. The theory no longer fits conditions.

A spirit of true humanitarianism must arise to counter

the spirit of inhumanity, which today is the ruling force in the world, and which threatens to destroy us.

Decisive action for the cause of maintaining peace must be undertaken and carried out without delay.

An End to Atomic Weapons

We live in a dark and frightening age. One reason for this is the part played by the ideology of inhumanity in our time.

We have been plunged into this situation by the achievements of science and technology, which have vastly increased the destructive power of the weapons used in the last two world wars. The use of such weapons has led to a sharp rise in inhuman actions and inhuman ideology.

We have submitted to this development without resistance. When the two world wars brought a new ruthlessness to warfare, so that any ship might be sunk by submarines and any city bombed by planes, public opinion did not rise up to denounce this growing inhumanity. There took place automatically a brutalization of sensibility on the part of individuals and nations. People avoided giving thought to the misery that this new type of warfare imposed. They accepted the fact that the numbers of human lives sacrificed now ran into the millions.

Any thoughtful analysis of what had happened and the manner in which we had come to accept it, was cut off by the appearance of atomic weapons, with the prospect they brought of still greater annihilation and still greater inhumanity.

The atomic bomb dropped upon the Japanese city of Hiroshima on August 6, 1945, provided a foretaste of the ravages and human misery that the widespread use of such weapons would produce. For now there was added, to the devastation produced by the tremendous explosive force, the effects of radioactivity, of enormous air pressure, and of the heat cast by giant conflagrations. People ran through the streets of Hiroshima like human torches, vainly seeking water in which to quench the flames.

We have also learned, from the fate of the Hiroshima survivors and their offspring, the deadly lingering effects of radiation that was not immediately fatal.

Today we have advanced so far in the development of all types of atomic weapons that their effects are more than a thousandfold that of the Hiroshima bomb —in other words, absolutely inconceivable. To consider waging war with such weapons presupposes an utterly inhuman ideology.

All nations, especially the ones that have atomic weapons at their disposal, must refuse even to talk of atomic war as a potential resort. But a good many of them will not realize that we are dealing with a spiritual and ethical problem. They think that peace or atomic war will go on being a purely political and military problem, and that the relevant decisions can be left to those who govern, the diplomats and generals.

For years, the banning of nuclear testing and the abolition of nuclear weapons has been discussed in this way, without result. If in the course of the negotiations the point was raised that use of these weapons is inconceivably inhuman, most of the delegates to the parleys would skirt the question. They believed that the possibility must be left open of deciding for atomic war.

Such thinking overlooks even the obvious military considerations: that there can scarcely be any real victory over the enemy in an atomic war. Neither of the two major opponents is significantly superior to the other. The defeated side can inflict such terrible damage upon the victor that victory will be meaningless.

We may categorically state that there is no practical problem existing between nations whose importance is in any proportion to the tremendous losses which must be expected in an atomic war. An atomic war for whatever cause is absolutely senseless. Nevertheless, a good many statesmen go on saying that in this or that case they would resort to the extreme measure, that is, to an atomic war. . . .

The possibility of an outbreak of atomic war between East and West in our time flows directly from the fear both sides have of a surprise attack by the other. Atomic weapons are surprise weapons. The aggressor will always command a considerable advantage.

The ideology of inhumanity, which is so prevalent in our times, is at the root of this dangerous fear. Trust among nations has been destroyed merely by the existence of atomic weapons.

We can find our way out of this crisis only by summoning up the insight and energy to exorcise from our minds the unlimited inhumanity that has taken possession of us, through the presence of atomic weapons. We must become conscious of our obligations to humanity, which demands the abolition of atomic weapons. Such abolition would in turn create an atmosphere in which nations could once again negotiate trustfully with one another.

Pessimists may doubt that such a spiritual and ethical conversion can take place. But why not? Humanitarianism corresponds to our true nature. As soon as we seriously reflect, we have no choice but to decide in favor of an ideology of humanitarianism.

In our efforts to return to humanitarianism, we can find the needed strength in the ethics of reverence for life. An ethics concerned only with the conduct of man toward other men does not possess the elemental force and the breadth of vision implicit in reverence for life. Concern solely with good actions between men obscures the need for combatting cruelty and killing in general. Yet the latter is what our horrible age demands. The ethics of reverence for life has arisen in our time; it is at home in our time and geared to the distresses and requirements of our time.

Let us then set about awakening a public that in any case instinctively draws back from the inhumanity of using atomic weapons.

The course of human history has reached the point today at which a prodigious political problem—prodigious because it involves the continued existence of humanity—can no longer be dealt with and solved by purely political methods. Ordinary political procedures have proved inadequate in the course of the past few years. A decision can be reached only on the basis of public opinion in the nations concerned. Public opinion must declare whether it is to stay caught in the ideology of inhumanity, which approves the retention of atomic weapons, or whether it wishes to adopt an ideology of humanitarianism and demand the abolition of such weapons.

The nations cannot continue to abide in that state of vapid indecision into which they have withdrawn, either from irresolution or from coercion by politicians. For far too long, these policies have been left to the judgment of politicians, and the voice of the people of the world has not been heard.

The command of the hour is that the people of the countries possessing atomic weapons make their voices heard. They must take over the responsibility and prove capable of the spiritual act of commitment to humanitarianism.

The salvation of mankind depends upon the success of such a policy. Lacking it, we are doomed to living in deepening misery, or to final annihilation.

This little book grew out of a proposal
which Gerald Götting made to me
during a visit to Lambaréné in August, 1961.

Albert Schweitzer